j92
JOSEPH

Sanford, William R.
(William Reynolds),
1927-

Chief Joseph, Nez
Perce warrior.

$14.95

DATE			

BAKER & TAYLOR

NATIVE AMERICAN LEADERS
OF THE WILD WEST

CHIEF JOSEPH

❖ Nez Percé Warrior ❖

William R. Sanford

ENSLOW PUBLISHERS, INC.

Bloy St. & Ramsey Ave.   P.O. Box 38
Box 777   Aldershot
Hillside, N.J. 07205   Hants GU12 6BP
U.S.A.   U.K.

Library of Congress Cataloging-in-Publication Data

Sanford, William R. (William Reynolds), 1927–
    Chief Joseph: Nez Percé warrior / William R. Sanford.
        p. cm. — (Native American leaders of the Wild West.)
    Includes bibliographical references and index.
    ISBN 0-89490-509-0
    1. Joseph, Nez Percé Chief, 1840–1904—Juvenile literature. 2. Nez Percé Indi-
ans—Biography—Juvenile literature. 3. Nez Percé Indians—Kings and
rulers—Juvenile literature. 4. Nez Percé Indians—History—Juvenile literature.
I. Title. II. Series: Sanford, William R. (William Reynolds), 1927– Native American
leaders of the Wild West.
E99.N5J587 1994
979′.004974′0092—dc20
[B]   93-41479
                                                                   CIP
                                                                    AC

Printed in the United States of America

10 9 8 7 6 5 4 3 2 1

Photo Credits: Montana Historical Society, pp. 6, 11, 12, 19, 36, 39, 41;
National Archives, pp. 16, 34; William R. Sanford, pp. 8, 14, 23, 28, 32, 35;
Smithsonian Institute, pp. 24, 30; Washington Historical Society, p. 21.

Cover Illustration: Paul Daly

CONTENTS

═══AUTHOR'S NOTE═══

This book tells the true story of the Nez Percé leader, Chief Joseph. Many mistakenly think the great warrior led all the Nez Percé. His true fame rests on his leadership of only a few hundred. During his long march toward freedom, the press raced to print stories about Chief Joseph. Some were made up, but others were true. The events described in this book all really happened.

In French, Nez Percé (pronounced Nay Pear Say) means "pierced nose." In the early 1800s, French trappers first met the tribe. A few of them wore dentalium shells through their noses. The practice was not common, but the name stuck anyway.

CHIEF JOSEPH LEADS
HIS PEOPLE TO WAR

Joseph and his brother Ollicutt returned to the Rocky Canyon camp. They had been gone for several days to butcher cattle. They learned that war with the white settlers had started. Shore Crossing, a member of White Bird's band, had killed four whites. Two years before, settlers had killed his father. Other members of the band taunted him. Why, they asked, didn't he kill his father's murderers. Shore Crossing set out to do just that. But he couldn't find the murderers. Instead, he killed four other Salmon River settlers. They were men who had done harm to the Nez Percé. Later, Joseph said, "I would have given my life if I could have undone the killing of white men by my people."[1]

Many Nez Percé from other bands fled. They feared the whites would blame them for the killings.[2] Joseph knew it didn't matter to which band Shore Crossing belonged. Whites would blame all the Nez Percé. Joseph led his band sixteen miles to White Bird Creek. There they would be safe from surprise attack. Within days Nez Percé warriors killed fourteen more settlers. The Army had to respond.

General Oliver O. Howard led the Army in the region. The general wired his superiors, "Think we shall make short work of it."[3] Howard sent Captain David Perry and ninety-two cavalrymen to attack the Nez Percé. Howard warned the captain: "You must not get whipped." Perry replied, "There is no danger of that."[4]

Perry and his cavalrymen rode seventy miles in sixteen hours. Outside the camp a Nez Percé scout gave

Joseph knew trouble with white settlers would be disastrous for the Nez Percé.

a warning coyote howl. The troops were coming. Joseph was ready. Soon after 4 A.M., June 17, 1877, light filled White Bird Canyon. A line of troopers four-abreast rode down the narrow pass. Every able-bodied Nez Percé lay in wait. Joseph still hoped to avoid trouble.[5] He sent a scout forward with a white flag of truce. The soldiers did not want to talk. One of them fired a shot. The battle had begun. Joseph commanded one end of the line; Ollicutt, the other. On the flanks, Little Runner attacked the soldiers' right. Two Moons fired down from high ground on the left. The Nez Percé warriors used their rifles with deadly accuracy. Behind them the old men shot their arrows over the front line's heads.

Both sides found cover in the rocks. Neither could dislodge the other. The Nez Percé gathered a herd of horses. They drove them into the soldiers' line. With the herd rode sixty of the fiercest warriors. These braves then opened fire from the soldiers' rear. Perry had to fall back. The retreat lasted for hours.

The troops fell back at a walk. At times the Nez Percé dashed close. Then the troops would stop and fire a volley. They repeated this tactic over and over. Often the soldiers stopped for stragglers to catch up. Sometimes soldiers stumbled into dead-end canyons. There the Nez Percé killed them, one by one. The running battle covered a dozen miles. It ended four miles from the town of Mount Idaho. A relief force came to aid the soldiers. Then the Nez Percé finally broke off the attack.

No Nez Percé died in the battle. Only three received wounds. The soldiers suffered thirty-four deaths. It was one of the biggest defeats of the U.S. Army by Native Americans. Outraged, Howard vowed to hunt down the Nez Percé.

Scouts gave warning of approaching soldiers. They used blankets, mirrors, and smoke signals.

A BACKGROUND FOR
LEADERSHIP

The Nez Percé's homeland included southeast
Washington, north central Idaho, and northeastern
Oregon. It was a vast area of mountains, plains, valleys,
and sagebrush plateaus. In the west, lofty peaks rose
thousands of feet toward the sky. Blue-green forests
covered their slopes. Even in summer, snowfields
covered their peaks. Mountain-rimmed lakes lay flat as
mirrors. Trout broke the surface, leaping for flies.
Clumps of sage dotted the foothills. Bunchgrass
carpeted the plateaus. The winds blew warm and dry.

Joseph was born in the summer of 1840. His
birthplace lay near the shores of Lake Wallowa in eastern
Oregon. His father Tuekas (Old Joseph) and mother
Arenoth were Christians. Ollicutt, his younger brother,
arrived two years later. As a child Joseph roamed the
village naked. He watched the women grind flour from

camas roots. He saw others using sharp stones to scrape the fat from the hides of deer and elk.

Once the sun set, the air grew chilly. The women built fires in front of the lodges. Young men made arrow points. Old women sewed beads on garments. Sometimes Joseph joined other children around the fire. Old warriors spoke of times past. They told ancient stories. At night Joseph stretched out under buffalo robes. The howls of the coyotes lulled him to sleep. When Joseph was five, he and his brother went to a mission school at Lapwai. He was too young to learn to read or write much English.

About 1850 some Nez Percé began to practice the Earth Mother or Dreamer religion. Its founder was the medicine man Smohalla. General Howard called him a "large-headed, hump-shouldered, odd little wizard."[1] The Nez Percé admired the prophet and followed his teaching. At times Smohalla had fits. When he passed out, he dreamed. Smohalla said that the Great Spirit revealed the future in dreams.

Smohalla taught that the Nez Percé should not adopt the ways of whites. They should not raise crops, nor live off white men's gifts. Doing so angered the Great Spirit. The earth was their sacred Mother. Smohalla compared plowing to cutting a mother's flesh. He said the Nez Percé should return to a simple life. Then, Smohalla promised, a great Native American leader would arise.

Chief Joseph stands before his tipi. The cone-shaped home stretched over a framework of lodge poles. It could be put up or taken down quickly.

He would drive out the whites. All the dead Native Americans would return to life.

When Joseph was nine or ten, he gained a new name. One day he stripped off his clothes. Without weapons he left the village. After a long climb, Joseph reached the top of a steep ridge. There he sat cross-legged and waited. With eyes closed he prayed to the Great Spirit.

All day and all night he waited. He did not eat or drink. The next morning Joseph fell asleep. In a dream he saw thunder coming closer. Joseph returned to his father's lodge. He had his new name: Hin-Mut-Too-Yah-Lat-Kekth. It meant "Thunder Rolling Over the Mountains."[2]

Joseph grew tall and handsome. As an adult he stood six-feet two-inches and weighed two hundred pounds. Joseph had black piercing eyes and a square chin. He wore his hair in two long braids over his shoulders. Joseph married for the first time when he was twenty-three. During his lifetime Joseph married four wives. In all, they bore him five daughters and four sons. All but two daughters died as infants. Joseph had no grandchildren.

Chief Joseph was tall and handsome. A big man, he stood six feet, two inches and weighed over 200 pounds.

JOSEPH DECIDES TO MOVE OR FIGHT

In May 1855, the governor of Washington Territory called a treaty council. Twenty-five hundred Nez Percé met at the council grounds at Walla Walla. The governor said he wanted to divide the land. The Nez Percé and whites would live apart. In June the chiefs signed a treaty. They would move to a 10,000 square mile reservation. It embraced most of their homeland.

The story of Chief Joseph centers about treaties between Native Americans and whites. These treaties reflected three ideas of whites: 1) Every tribe had one chief. 2) That chief ruled his tribe. 3) The tribe owned the land upon which it lived. All three ideas were false. Only rarely did a tribe unite under one chief. Most tribes had many bands. Each band had its own leader. He could not sell the band's land. No tribe thought it owned the land.

The whites did not recognize this way of life. They

often dealt with the leader of a band. They acted as though he were the chief of the whole tribe. They got him to sign a treaty. The treaty allowed the whites to gain the land they wanted.

In June 1860, a miner found gold on Nez Percé lands. Soon, over 18,000 whites flooded in. In 1863 the whites asked the Nez Percé to sign a new treaty. It cut the tribe's reservation to six hundred square miles. Old Joseph and two dozen other chiefs refused. Fifty-two Nez Percé, led by Chief Lawyer, did sign the treaty. Twenty-five or more of them signed in place of the dissenting chiefs. They made it look like the entire tribe had agreed to the treaty.

The treaty required the Nez Percé to go to the Lapwai Reservation within a year. All Nez Percé must

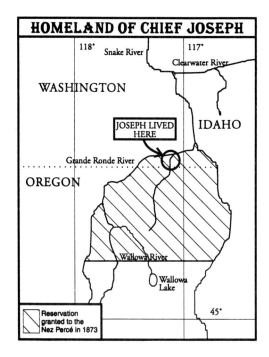

The Nez Percé homeland occupied what are now Washington, Oregon, and Idaho.

move—whether they signed or not! Those who did not sign called the treaty the "Thief Treaty." They refused to leave their lands. Young Joseph said, "If we ever owned the land, we own it still, for we never sold it."[1]

In 1871 Old Joseph knew he was dying. He told his son, "Never forget my dying words. This country holds your father's body. Never sell the bones of your father and mother."[2] Young Joseph became Chief Joseph. In March 1875, President Grant declared the Wallowa Valley open for settlement by whites. Joseph's band of forty-five families spent the summer in its Wallowa homeland. Two companies of troops kept peace between the Nez Percé and the settlers.

The next summer, settlers A. B. Findley and Wells McNall tracked five missing horses to a Nez Percé camp. In an argument McNall wrestled with Wind Blowing for possession of a gun. During the fight Findley opened fire, killing the young Nez Percé. The white men fled. Chief Joseph restrained his angry warriors. He got in touch with Indian Agent John Monteith. Monteith promised the whites would go on trial. A jury found Findley not guilty. The patience of the Nez Percé stretched thin.

The Department of the Interior decided in January 1877 to move Chief Joseph's people onto a reservation. They were ready to use force. They asked him to move by April 1. Joseph and the anti-treaty chiefs agreed to meet at Lapwai to talk with General Howard. Howard's

After the death of his father, Young Joseph became Chief Joseph.

first campaign had been against the Seminoles in Florida. Howard took part in more than twenty Civil War battles. In 1862, he lost his right arm at the Battle of Fair Oaks. Two years later he led a wing of Sherman's army during the "March to the Sea." After the Civil War he served as president of Howard University. Howard tried to be a friend to the Nez Percé. He had written the Secretary of War, "Possibly Congress can be induced to let these really peaceable Indians have this poor valley for their own."[3]

The meeting took place early in May. The Nez Percé chose the shaman Too-hool-hool-sote as their spokesman. The medicine man challenged Howard. He said, "The Great Spirit Chief made the world as it is and as he wanted it. He made a part of it for us to live on. I do not see where you get the authority to say that we shall not live where he placed us."[4]

Howard lost his temper. The general marched Too-hool-hool-sote to the guardhouse. Howard told the others that they must move within thirty days. If not, he would drive them onto the reservation. Joseph asked for time to gather his livestock. General Howard refused. Now Joseph had to decide whether to move or fight.

COMING TO LAPWAI
RESERVATION

General Howard warned Joseph. "If you let the time run over one day, the soldiers will be there to drive you onto the reservation. The cattle outside the reservation will fall into the hands of the white men."[1]

Joseph told the general, "War can be avoided and ought to be avoided. I want no war. My people have always been friends of the white man. Why are you in such a hurry?"[2]

Joseph had given his word. His Nez Percé would move to the reservation before the deadline. Joseph led only the Wallowa Valley band. Other non-treaty bands followed Chiefs Looking Glass, White Bird, Rainbow, and Eagle-From-the-Light. Joseph could not speak for them. By day the young men rounded up their livestock. At night some warriors raged at Joseph in council. They said the Nez Percé were acting out of fear. They reminded Joseph that here his father's bones rested. He had promised not to sell the land. Now he was giving it away. Joseph's band joined the others in the removal to Lapwai.

Nez Percé riders combed a million acres of hills, meadowlands, valleys, and ridges. They drove the cattle and horses toward the river. Along the way, the whites moved in. They stole stray horses. They slaughtered cows, taking only choice cuts. They carried away colts and calves. Over two weeks, whites stole thousands of head of cattle. When Joseph complained, white sheriffs did nothing to help the Nez Percé. At night the councils continued. Some argued there were too many whites to

A Nez Percé encampment.

fight and win. Others said that if the Nez Percé won battles, the whites would then leave them alone.

To reach the reservation, the Nez Percé had to cross the Snake River with their belongings and herds. The quarter-mile-wide river was in flood. Trunks from mountain trees tumbled end over end in the raging brown current. It looked impossible to cross. Two companies of soldiers camped nearby in the hills. They offered no help.

On horseback Joseph directed the first crossing. The Nez Percé piled up lodge skins, clothing, and food. They placed them on rafts and covered them with elk skins. From each corner a rope led to a horseman. The riders kicked their mounts into the river. The current pulled them almost two hundred yards downstream. At last rafts and riders reached the other side safely.

It was time for the women and children to cross. The riders lashed them to rafts and fought their way across. The livestock crossed last. Riders first encircled the horses. At a signal they whooped and charged into the herd. In a controlled stampede, the horses dashed into the river. When they reached the other side, riders rounded them up. The cattle crossed in the same manner. The current carried away the smaller and weaker animals. On the other side, riders drove the herds to higher ground. There they posted armed guards. The Nez Percé did not lose a single person in the crossing.

Ten days remained before General Howard's

deadline. They camped in Rocky Canyon, almost on the reservation's edge. Here the Nez Percé would spend their last ten days of freedom. They dried their packs in the bright June sun. Joseph ordered dances, races, and games. He hoped the talk of war had ended.[3]

Warriors dressed in colorful aprons. They hunted with rifles and pistols whenever they could get them by trade or capture.

JOSEPH LEADS THE WAY THROUGH IDAHO

War did follow, however. The Nez Percé won the first battle at White Bird Canyon. The fighting did not stop there. The press urged General Howard to avenge the Army's defeat. On June 22, Howard left Fort Lapwai with four hundred soldiers and one hundred scouts. When the troops came near, the Nez Percé fled. Their herds swam the swift Salmon River. Women, children, and goods floated across on rafts. The soldiers crossed the Salmon on July 1st. The Nez Percé recrossed the river twenty-five miles north at Craig's Ferry. On July 6, the troops tried to cross at the same point. They failed. Howard doubled back to White Bird Canyon. His futile pursuit had lasted eight days.

Before he left Fort Lapwai, Howard had received a false report. It said Looking Glass was planning to attack the whites. Howard sent two cavalry companies to the

Clearwater River to arrest the chief. Under a white flag, two Nez Percé rode out to meet the soldiers. They assured the soldiers that Looking Glass's band was peaceful. Without warning, an Army scout shot one of the Nez Percé. As fighting spread, the Nez Percé scattered. Joseph learned of the attack while being pursued himself. He led his Nez Percé to join Looking Glass's band. On the shores of the Clearwater River, they rested, repaired equipment, and hunted.

Howard reached the Clearwater on July 11. His column stretched for two miles. He headed north on a

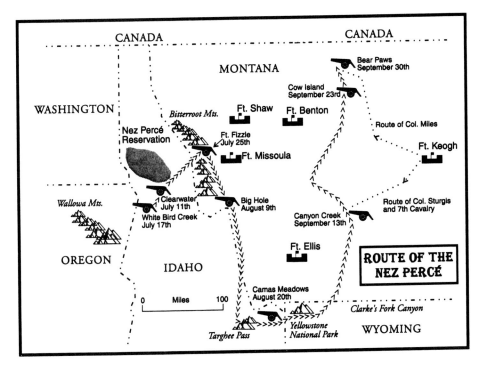

The journey of the Nez Percé covered hundreds of miles.

Looking Glass, shown here, was a leader of the non-treaty Nez Percé. His band joined with Joseph's in the long trek to escape army pursuit.

plateau high above the east bank of the river. There the troops stumbled upon the Nez Percé camp. They caught the Nez Percé by surprise. The soldiers opened fire with cannons and Gatling guns. The Nez Percé fired back from behind rock barricades. Joseph led the Nez Percé in flanking movements and charges. He said, "If we die in battle, it is good. It is good dying for your rights, for your country."[1] The fighting lasted all day and into the next. That afternoon the Nez Percé withdrew. They had suffered four dead; the soldiers, fifteen.

Joseph knew the soldiers would continue to pursue his people.[2] He decided to lead them from their beloved land of winding waters. On July 14 the Nez Percé took the Lolo Trail. It lead across the Bitterroot Mountains to Montana. The Nez Percé thought "Montana people are not our enemies. The war we leave here in Idaho."[3] Joseph picked the medicine man, Pile of Clouds, as his war chief. Pile of Clouds led the Nez Percé on their march. For two weeks they wound their way through dense forests and barren high ground. At Lolo Hot Springs they paused to rest and bathe. They sent messengers to the Flatheads to ask for help. The answer came back quickly. The tribe would not help them.

Scouts reported that troops blocked their way. Soldiers had built a crude fort at the end of a narrow pass. The chiefs formed an escape plan. The Nez Percé went to the stockade under a white flag. For three days Joseph, Looking Glass, and White Bird talked with Captain Charles Rawn. Joseph told him, "We have no hatred in our hearts for any white man. We are fighting only those who drove us from our home."[4]

While Joseph talked, the young braves built a ramp up the side of a cliff. From its top a goat trail led above and around the fort. One morning Joseph sat on his horse outside the stockade. As he talked with Captain Rawn, the Nez Percé escaped up the trail. After that the soldiers called their stockade Fort Fizzle.

THE DISASTROUS
ATTACK AT BIG HOLE

The Nez Percé chiefs held a council. They knew Sitting Bull and the Sioux had found safety in Canada. They too would go there. Most of the chiefs wished to head north to "the Old Woman's country" at once. Looking Glass insisted on heading south. The Nez Percé would pass through the country of the Crows. He was sure that the Crows would help them. Joseph and the others agreed to try Looking Glass's plan. The Nez Percé released captives to spread the word. They hoped to cross the Bitterroot Valley in peace. For ten days they moved south, trading as they went. Some Nez Percé stole flour from settlers. Joseph made them pay for it with horses.

On August 7, the Nez Percé stopped to camp by the Big Hole River. Pile of Clouds urged the Nez Percé to move on quickly. He said, "Death is on our trail."[1] He warned that soldiers in Montana were the same as those in Idaho. The young men wanted to stop to hunt. Looking Glass decided. They would stay. Here, at the Place of Ground Squirrels, the prairie grass was lush. Dark green pines lined the hillsides. The Nez Percé felled trees to make new lodge poles. Soon, eighty-nine lodges lined the river bank.

At dawn two days later, Colonel John Gibbon found the sleeping camp. His two-hundred-man force from Fort Shaw attacked from the north, northwest, and west. He told his men to take no prisoners. The Nez Percé stumbled from their lodges. Rifle fire cut them down. One of Joseph's wives was among the slain. Joseph led a charge across the river to rescue the horses. Barefoot, he wore only a shirt and blanket. He returned to carry screaming children to safety by the river bank. Looking Glass and White Bird rallied the warriors. "Now is our time to fight," they shouted.[2] Their return fire killed many soldiers. During the battle a group of Nez Percé captured the army supply train. Now they had 20,000 rounds of rifle ammunition.

After four hours Gibbon retreated to a nearby plateau. With a dozen men Ollicutt poured fire into Gibbon's force. A grief-stricken Joseph ordered the Nez Percé to pack their lodges and leave. The women wailed for the slain. The dead included fifty women and children. Yellow Wolf reported, "Only twelve of the fighting men were lost in that battle. But our best were left there."[3]

The Nez Percé carried off their wounded on travois.

The heavy-laden army column found the going hard. They could not catch up with the fleeing Nez Percé.

They knew the Army would not care for them. Joseph led the Nez Percé south. As they fled, angry warriors killed whites. They slew five in a raid to get new horses. Five drivers died when the Nez Percé captured a wagon train.

On August 20, General Howard was just one day behind the Nez Percé. Ollicutt led two dozen warriors in a nighttime raid. They stampeded two hundred mules and delayed Howard one more day. General Howard then sent cavalry to hold Targhee Pass. When the cavalry reached the pass, there was no sign of the Nez Percé. The troops left the pass unguarded. The Nez Percé turned north through the pass a day later. The way into the Yellowstone country was now open.

7

THE NEZ PERCÉ FLEE TOWARD CANADA

The Nez Percé entered the Yellowstone country on August 23, 1877. A captured prospector, John Shively, guided them up the Madison River. Birch, aspen, and beech trees flamed golden. The Nez Percé marveled at the colored terraces, pools of boiling water, and geysers. They watched as Old Faithful erupted every sixty-five minutes. Yellowstone had become the first U.S. national park in 1872. In Yellowstone the Nez Percé captured nine tourists. One was a thirteen-year-old girl. One of the captives described Joseph. He was "...somber and silent ... grave and dignified. He looked like a chief."[1] A few days later the Nez Percé met a second party of tourists. They killed one of them.

Joseph knew that Howard's troops were close behind. Early in September his advance scouts ran into a unit of the Seventh Cavalry. The Nez Percé were almost

Chief Joseph of the Nez Percé was described by a captive tourist as "... somber and silent ... grave and dignified. He looked like a chief."

surrounded. Soldiers closed both ends of the Yellowstone Valley. Two companies of cavalry waited to the north. General Crook's fifteen cavalry companies lay to the east and southeast. On September 8, the Nez Percé began a retreat to the south. Soon they milled their ponies to confuse their tracks. Then they headed north across the valley and into the mountains. In the canyons, the rocky walls were close together. Two horses abreast could scarcely pass. The Nez Percé left the mountains near Canyon Creek. Once more the Nez Percé had outfoxed their pursuers. Weary, they paused briefly to rest.

Looking Glass went to ask for help from the Crow nation. The Mountain Crows said they would remain neutral. The River Crows sided with the whites. No one would help the Nez Percé. Instead, when they could, they stole horses from the Nez Percé. Yellow Wolf exclaimed, "I do not understand how the Crows could think to help the soldiers. Some Nez Percé in our band had helped them whip the Sioux who came against them only a few snows before."[2]

To get to Canyon Creek, the cavalry rode sixty miles in one day. On September 13, Joseph's lookouts waved red blankets. It was a signal that the soldiers were near. The women and children fled up the Canyon Creek gorge. The Nez Percé blocked the way with rocks and fallen trees. For two days, the warriors fought a rear guard action. Crow scouts stole forty Nez Percé horses.

The next day the Nez Percé captured fresh horses from the camp of Crow Chief Dumb Bull.

For a week the Nez Percé moved north. They covered thirty or more miles a day. On September 23, they reached the Missouri River. At Cow Island the Nez Percé raided an army supply station. They took flour, sugar, coffee, pots, and pans. The guard wired, "Colonel: Chief Joseph is here. He says he will surrender for two hundred bags of sugar. I told him to surrender without the sugar. He took the sugar and will not surrender. What will I do? Michael Foley."[3]

The weary chiefs slowed their pace. For four more days they drifted north. Joseph received no word from his scouts of any pursuit. He began to feel secure. His band might reach Canada after all.

The Nez Percé wondered how the soldiers always knew where they were going. They did not know that word of their movements went by telegraph and fast riders from army post to army post.

JOSEPH SURRENDERS AT LAST

At Snake Creek, Joseph's weary band set up camp. The site was open to attack from three sides. Pile of Clouds urged Joseph to move on at once. Canada lay only one day's march to the north across rolling plains. Joseph said no. Half the horses were lame. Many aged could no longer ride the travois. Warriors drooped in their saddles. The Nez Percé must rest and regain strength. He hoped they had time. He knew the "singing wires," as the Nez Percé called the telegraph,[1] would tell the soldiers where they were.

On the morning of September 30, the Nez Percé began to pack and gather their horses. At 8:00 A.M. a herd boy rode in with the warning. Soldiers approached in two lines. Colonel Nelson Miles' force had ridden hard for four days. Joseph dashed across the creek to save the herds.

The Seventh Cavalry attacked from the south. The warriors poured rifle fire into the soldiers. Their leader, Captain Owen Hale and twenty-two other soldiers fell dead. Forty-two more received wounds. The Second Cavalry swung west. It captured most of the Nez Percé herd. When the battle began Joseph was across the creek from the camp. He and seventy warriors found themselves cut off from the main camp. Miles sent the Fifth Infantry forward in a charge. The warriors drove them back. That afternoon an attack reached the edge of the camp. Again the Nez Percé drove them back. The soldiers then made a ring around the camp. The battle became a siege.

Sitting Bull and the Hunkpapa Sioux had found refuge in Canada some years before. The Nez Percé hoped they could do the same.

The bitter cold of the Montana winter caused hardship for the soldiers and Nez Percé. The lack of housing and clothing caused many of Joseph's people to freeze to death.

During the night five inches of snow fell. The Nez Percé spent the hours of darkness digging. The warriors dug rifle pits. The women scooped out tunnels and trenches with knives and pans. Six warriors hurried north. They would ask the 2,000 Sioux of Sitting Bull to come to their rescue. They never reached him. Members of a local tribe killed all six.

At noon the next day the soldiers raised a white flag. They asked Chief Joseph to come to talk with Colonel Miles. The colonel asked Joseph to sit by the fire and talk things over. Joseph asked that the Nez Percé be allowed to return to the Wallowa Valley. Miles demanded unconditional surrender. When Joseph refused, Miles made him a prisoner. The next morning the Nez Percé traded their prisoner, Lieutenant Jerome, for Joseph.

The siege lasted two more days. On October 5, General Howard arrived with his troops. Toward noon two of Howard's Nez Percé scouts carried a white flag to Joseph's camp. Again they asked him to surrender.

When Joseph realized there would be no reaching Canada, he chose to save his people further hardship and surrendered at Snake Creek.

Joseph refused. The scouts came a second time, bringing Miles' promise. He would send the Nez Percé back to their reservation. Joseph thought Miles had agreed to his peace terms.[2]

Joseph rode out slowly to meet the soldiers. He wrapped himself in a gray blanket. Bullets had torn his leggings and shirt. Other bullets had scarred his forehead and wrists. He offered his rifle to Howard, who waved it to Miles.

A Nez Percé scout, Captain John, reported Chief Joseph's words to Colonel Miles:

> *"I am tired of fighting. Our chiefs are killed. Looking Glass is dead. Too-hool-hool-sote is dead. Our old men are all dead. . . [Ollicutt is dead]. It is cold and we have no blankets. The little children are freezing to death. My people, some of them, have run away to the hills. . . . No one knows where they are—perhaps freezing to death. I want to have time to look for my children and see how many of them I can find. Maybe I shall find them among the dead. . . . I am tired. My heart is sick and sad. From where the sun now stands, I will fight no more forever."[3]*

LIFE IN CAPTIVITY

Joseph had begun his march with perhaps 750 Nez Percé. In eleven weeks they traveled 1,700 miles. Along the route, 120 met their deaths. Only eighty-seven men surrendered. With them were 184 women and 147 children. Two hundred and thirty Nez Percé escaped after the battle on Snake Creek. White Bird and Yellow Wolf led small bands north. Small groups made their way back to Lapwai.

General Sherman ordered Miles to break his word. The Nez Percé were not to return home. Instead, he sent them eight hundred miles to Fort Lincoln, North Dakota. The people of Bismarck knew of Joseph's efforts to reach freedom in Canada. On November 16, they greeted Joseph as a hero. They held a dinner and dance for the Nez Percé. A band played in the town square.

The Army took the Nez Percé by train to Fort

Leavenworth, Kansas. Their camp was in a swampy area beside the Missouri River. Within months twenty-one died of malaria. In July 1878, the Nez Percé moved to the parched Quapaw Reservation. It was in the Indian Territory (now Oklahoma). They called it "the Hot Place." By October forty-seven more died. In January 1879, Joseph met in Washington, D.C., with President Hayes. Hayes refused to allow Joseph's people to return home. By June only 370 of them remained. They moved again to the nearby Ponca Reservation. There the Nez Percé tried to raise grain and grow vegetables. They had no houses. Their tipis offered poor shelter from the rains. The children continued to die. By 1881 Joseph's group had shrunk to 328.

Joseph never returned to live in his beloved Wallowa region. In July 1904, Chief Joseph was a member of the Nez Percé camp at Nespelem, Washington. This was to be Chief Joseph's last encampment.

Many took up Joseph's cause. By May 1884, Congress had before it fourteen petitions supporting the Nez Percé. They came from the Indian Rights Association, churches, and women's groups. In May 1885, the U.S. permitted the remaining Nez Percé to return to the Northwest. One hundred and eighteen went to the Nez Percé reservation in Idaho. There the other bands greeted them warmly. Settlers in Idaho still feared Chief Joseph. Because of this, the Army took him and 150 others to the Colville Reservation, in Washington State. The Nez Percé were thinly clad. They had no cattle, no tools, not enough food. In December, Joseph led his band in a final move. They settled in the Nespelem Valley, Washington. He then was about 45. Joseph was still deep-chested and broad-shouldered. He wore his hair in braids. Except for moccasins, he wore white man's clothes. Visitors found him friendly but reserved.[1]

In 1889 Joseph refused to accept 160 acres at Lapwai. He would only accept land at Wallowa. In 1897 Buffalo Bill invited Joseph to visit New York as his guest. In New York he rode with Generals Howard and Miles at the dedication of Grant's tomb. Miles had become a friend of Joseph. He tried without success to help the Nez Percé. Three years later Joseph visited his beloved Wallowa Valley. Twenty-three years had elapsed since his flight. Tearfully he visited his father's grave. Joseph stared into the reflections at Wallowa Lake. He had seen with his own eyes. There was no land left there for his people. The whites had taken it all and refused to sell him any.[2]

On September 21, 1904, Chief Joseph sat before the fire at Nespelem. He suffered a fatal heart attack. The agency physician Dr. Edwin Latham said, "Joseph died of a broken heart."[3]

Today the Nez Percé are still divided. Some live on the Colville Reservation, near Joseph's grave. Others live on the Nez Percé Reservation. The tribe has about 3,500 on its rolls.[4] About a third live off the reservation.[5]

Chief Joseph is remembered and revered by the Nez Percé on both reservations. He gave much to his people. He worked hard so that whites and Nez Percé could get along and live together "with one sky above."

Chief Joseph's grave is on the Colville Reservation in Washington. Today, some Nez Percé live there, while others are at the Nez Percé Agency in Idaho.

SMT MEMORIAL LIBRARY
50 NORTH MAIN ST.
SUFFIELD, CONN. 06078

NOTES BY CHAPTER

Chapter 1

1. C. Fayne Porter, *Our Indian Heritage* (Philadelphia: Chilton, 1964), p. 148.

2. Francis Haines, *The Nez Percé: Tribesmen of the Columbia Plateau* (Norman: University of Oklahoma Press, 1955), p. 249.

3. Benjamin Capps, *The Great Chiefs* (New York: Time-Life, 1975), p. 169.

4. Capps, p. 169.

5. Helen A. Howard, *Saga of Chief Joseph* (Lincoln: University of Nebraska, 1978), p. 163.

Chapter 2

1. H. Howard, p. 85.

2. Porter, p. 145.

Chapter 3

1. Jason Hook, *American Indian Warrior Chiefs* (New York: Sterling, 1989), p. 112.

2. Hook, p. 113.

3. Oliver O. Howard, *Chief Joseph: His Pursuit and Capture* (Boston: Lee & Shephard, 1881), p. 29.

4. Alvin M. Josephy, Jr., *The Nez Percé Indians and the Opening of the Northwest* (New Haven: Yale, 1965), p. 501.

Chapter 4

1. Haines, p. 242.

2. Ibid.

3. Russell Davis and Brent Ashabranner, *Chief Joseph: War Chief of the Nez Percé* (New York: McGraw-Hill, 1962), p. 39.

Chapter 5

1. Merrill D. Beal, *"I Will Fight No More Forever"* (Seattle: University of Washington, 1963), p. 74.

2. Shannon Garst, *Chief Joseph of the Nez Percé* (New York: Julian Messner, 1963), p. 149.

3. Beal, p. 83.

4. Garst, p. 150.

Chapter 6

1. Capps, p. 178.

2. Capps, p. 180.

3. Haines, p. 293.

Chapter 7

1. Mrs. George F. Cowan, "Reminiscences of Pioneer Life," *Contributions: Historical Society of Montana IV* (1903), p. 1–73.

2. L.V. McWhorter, *Yellow Wolf: His Own Story* (Caldwell, Ida.: Caxton Printers, 1940), p. 194.

3. Beal, p. 203.

Chapter 8

1. Davis and Ashabranner, p. 156.

2. H. Howard, p. 329.

3. H. Howard, p. 330.

Chapter 9

1. H. Howard, p. 356.

2. Josephy, p. 643.

3. H. Howard, p. 367.

4. Clifford E. Trafzer, *The Nez Percé* (New York: Chelsea House, 1992), p. 105.

5. Josephy, p. 643.

GLOSSARY

anti-treaty—The bands of Nez Percé who did not sign the Treaty of 1863 (known as the "Thief Treaty").

band—A subdivision of a tribe, sometimes only a few dozen in number.

chief—A leader of a band or tribe; often a chief was limited to a specific role, such as leadership in war.

council—A meeting of the adults in a tribe; all warriors had the right to express their opinions.

Dreamer—The religion of the anti-treaty Nez Percé; it taught that the Gods revealed truth through dreams.

Indian agent—The representative of the Indian Bureau on a reservation; the Nez Percé agent was chosen by the Presbyterian Church and ratified by the government.

Gatling guns—An early form of machine gun with many barrels; when cranked, Gatling guns rotated and fired rapidly.

lodge—The home of the Nez Percé; lodges were made of hide stretched over many poles.

medicine dream—Young Nez Percé deprived themselves of sleep and food. When exhausted, they fell asleep and dreamed. They believed the gods spoke to them in their dreams.

Old Woman's country—A name given to Canada, then ruled by Queen Victoria of the United Kingdom.

plateau—A large flat-topped hill or region.

rear guard action—A fight designed to slow up pursuit.

reservation—An area set aside by the U.S. government to be the permanent home of a group of Native Americans.

scouts—Skilled frontiersmen, scouts served as lookouts, read tracks, found trails, and located game.

shaman—A Native American priest; shamans often combined foretelling the future and practicing medicine.

treaty—An agreement between two governments; often treaties between Native Americans and whites dealt with the sale of land.

tribe—A large group of Native Americans speaking a common language and living in the same area.

troopers—Another name for mounted soldiers or cavalrymen.

warrior—An adult Native American fighting man.

MORE GOOD READING ABOUT
CHIEF JOSEPH

Beal, Merrill. *"I Will Fight No More Forever."* Seattle: University of Washington, 1963.

Burt, Olive. *Chief Joseph: Boy of the Nez Percé.* Indianapolis: Bobbs-Merrill, 1967.

Garst, Shannon. *Chief Joseph of the Nez Percé.* New York: Julian Messner, 1953.

Gidley, M. *Kopet, A Documentary Narrative of Chief Joseph's Last Years.* Seattle: University of Washington, 1981.

Haines, Francis. *The Nez Percé: Tribesmen of the Columbia Plateau.* Norman, Okla.: University of Oklahoma, 1955.

Hook, Jason. *American Indian Warrior Chiefs.* New York: Sterling, 1989.

Howard, Helen A. *Saga of Chief Joseph.* Lincoln, Neb.: University of Nebraska, 1979.

Josephy, Alvin, Jr. *The Nez Percé Indians and the Opening of the Northwest.* New Haven: Yale, 1965.

Porter, C. Fayne. *Our Indian Heritage.* Philadelphia: Chilton, 1964.

Trafzer, Clifford E. *The Nez Percé.* New York: Chelsea House, 1992.

INDEX